T0370324

Reflections

Volume 1

Phillip Andrew Griffin Adams Jr.

authorHOUSE®

AuthorHouse™
1663 Liberty Drive
Bloomington, IN 47403
www.authorhouse.com
Phone: 1-800-839-8640

First published by AuthorHouse 5/28/2010

ISBN: 978-1-4520-1547-7 (sc)

Library of Congress Control Number: 2010905730

Printed in the United States of America
Bloomington, Indiana

This book is printed on acid-free paper.

DEDICATED TO: THE HAITI TRAGEDY
& OMAHA MALL TRAGEDY.

<u>Notes:</u>
*I GIVE SPECIAL THANKS FIRST & FOREMOST TO
GOD FOR WITHOUT HIM, I COULDN'T HAVE DONE
THIS & TO STEPHANIE MULLINS FOR THROUGH
HER SHINE, MINE WAS NOT HARD TO FIND. AND
TO MY DAUGHTER ASIA,WITH LOVE ALWAYS*

POETRY WITH LOVE.

TABLE OF CONTENTS

THE DEDICATION

Dedicated to my daughter Asia Cheyann Smith Adams, my mother Cardine L. Jordan, my sister Emily Y. Adams, Phyllis J. Adams, Christopher Armstrong-my brother to whom I love dearly, Leslie & Marlette Jordan to whom I love and will always appreciate what they've done for me.

To Octavia, someone who's very dear to my heart the sister who is very near and dear to me & who I wish nothing but the best for. And last but not least, to the woman who stood by my side & who has made this so much easier Stephanie D. Mullins.

Special dedication to Emily Yvette & Phyllis J. Adams and also to my little nephew James, you've all made this a journey that has been fulfilled by the, love that all have given me and
THIS IS THE REASON FOR REFLECTIONS.

THE AUTHOR

PAGE REFLECTS

*I*NSPIRATIONS

LOUD VOICES CLAMMERING THRU MY EARS, A DESIRED
FEELING OF KNOWING WHAT'S COMING NEAR, A NEED
TO FEEL YOU A NEED TO HEAR YOU A NEED TO SEE YOU
A NEED TO BE APART OF YOU.
WISHING FOR ONE DAY THAT WE COULD AT LEAST
TOUCH HANDS.
AN INSPIRED FEELING YOU GIVE TO ME, THE
INSPIRATION YOU GIVE TO ME AS A MAN,
LUSTRIOUS AND SMOOTH IS THE VISIONS I SEE
WHEN I CLOSE MY EYES AND THINK OF YOU SMILING,
LAUGHING, CARESSING EMBRACING REACHING BUT
NOT SEEKING GRASPING AND LONGING TO KEEP
SPEAKING FOR ALL THESE THINGS YOU HAVE DONE IN
FRONT OF ME THEY EXPRESS YOUR DESIRES TO TEACH
TO REACH TO PREACH TO MY SOUL.
YOU HAVE INSPIRED A YOUNG BOY TO A GROWN MAN
AND THE INSPIRATION YOU'RE GIVING TO ME NOW
LEADS ME TO BRING FORTH UNDERSTANDING TO
THOSE WHO DON'T UNDERSTAND.
OH HOW I SAVOR THE SWEET TENDER MOMENTS
THAT YOU EMBRACE THAT YOU TAUGHT THAT YOU
LOVED THAT YOU GAVE THAT YOU WILL ALWAYS GIVE
FOR WITHOUT YOU I WAS SOOO ALL ALONE BUT YOU
HAVE LEFT ME TO UNDERSTAND THAT THROUGH ANY
NATION THERE WILL ALWAYS BE GENERATIONS THAT
WILL NEED SUPPORT AND INSPIRATION.

THIS IS DEDICATED TO THE YOUTH OF AMERICA!

ANATOMY

Your anatomy; has been blessed
By grace and praised by the human eye,
You have brightened the sky with one smile you are a rose in the garden
of life and your aroma is candy to the nose, the structure of curves and
firmness of flesh, add nothing and take away less, your anatomy is a
touch of reality and a mist of morning dew, and a mixture of shallow
water running all over me, I rise like the sun and fade like cloudy days,
I am by all means entrapped in your anatomy' for the walk of beauty
is right in front of me, it's the shape of heaven and the glory of all that
God has created, you are the anatomy that has captured my eyes and
embraced my heart and showed me what life is and already was, but
the anatomy is always appreciated by me.

BLACK RAIN

Black rain".
Falls upon my face
It traces dirt down my cheek
And leaves dampness on my feet
The rain drops are warm and they caress
me with each touch and cleanse
me with every brush
because black rain is my
reason and it's life to
my soul" it's the food and
the drink to which I
have thirsted for" oh black rain
your wash has soothed
me from head to toe, I am
released through pleasures
of nature's presents and
earths wisdom lets us know,
for black rain cleanses and "
purifies my soul.

ALL IS FAIR IN LOVE....

All is fair in love, the games we shared,

The hearts we broke' the reasons we told' and the seconds we've
booked cause all is fair in love, the words we say, and the glare in
your eyes when we share that first look,
The grime we've spread and the dirt we've took, the punch from
life when your heart got shook,
All is fair in love, from the sign of your name or the false state to
another mans claim,
The part in your heart when the water puts out the flame, Cause all
is fair in love,
When the river rises to the break of a flood, rearranging your life,
and changing the brisk wake of all falls,
Hiding in your tears but not crawling, but walking to the point of
love's hollow walls.

Cause all is fair in love, when your wish becomes a dream, or your
talk becomes a scream,
Cause all is fair in love, when your wake becomes the dawn,
Or your shine becomes dark. Cause love is here and sometimes
there, but that's
Why all in love is fair.

20 Back

20 Years '' and all I heard was hello,
a knock on the door and a kiss good-bye before you go,
20Years ''
And I haven't ever seen you cry, shed one tear'' or watch my body die,
20Years
And your love has never shown grace not by touch, or wash of my
sorrow from your lies,
And it feels so rough to watch 'the night as it just passes by, 20Years;
and it's tight through the storm and rain as I count all the day's of my
life, cause it's been 20 years ; inside the fire,
I've hidden in the bitter flame''
cried out loud and embraced all my feelings, but it's been 20 years…
Since I've heard myself shout, and the 20 years I've lost 'I could have
lived my life,
And I just try too hard'' so instead I wish my 20 years were never gone.

Beautiful

OH my love you are beautiful"

Your skin is bronze and it glows underneath the rays of the sun;

Your eyes are foot prints in the moon"

And the stars get lost whenever they see you,
Your breasts are soft like honey melon dew"

And your beauty is more than just physical, I get captured in your touch'

And the long conversation lingers in the rush.

You are beautiful,

by more than just looks' your essence is a blessing and it entices my intellect;

your tongue embraces my ears and your passion has drew us near,

I have been massaged by your mind and caressed in your dreams; I see beauty in everything that you do,

And I know real beauty whenever I'm with you.

$\mathcal{S}$OUL CONFESSIONS

Can I elaborate the things I see in you,
You're more special then you could have
Ever knew" you have obtained the degree of strength in which no one
has ever came near
You have formed the praise to wants that no man should ever give. You
are the light that shines from the sun that sits up above" I continue
the rise of moonlight and I pretend to share my life with you, I stroll
through daydreams and open my eyes to your smiling face" I have
journeyed a thousand miles and my heart has fallen to a dark and
romantic time" I am trapped by your web and I can not hold back
what is on my mind, but yet I can see the storm of emotions that lives
in your eyes because the conversing of what is real and the things I
truly feel, I am but a man in this my hearts reveals, I have seen your
taste of love and my breath you did steal

$\mathcal{S}$HINE

Let me express what I feel for you'
You have cared for my heart and made it apart of you,
And you have kidnapped my emotions and made them brandnew"
You took my spirit and made it shine,
For through your glow' mines was easy to find,
Because sex wasn't the issue'
It was all about the time, to form my expression' and share what
was on my mind,
Let me travel through your thoughts"
And listen to every line,
Can you accept my affection"
And erase all my grime, let me journey through your world"
And lead you as if you were blind, because to push me away would
blow my mind,
For the walk with you is soothing to me like wine"
I can express my words in so many ways,
because your true beauty comes through your touch:
the way you make me feel, when you open your mouth because
from your blue eyes to mines,
you always know what to say to make me shine.

BUT WILL I LISTEN.

MY CHILD CRY'S TO BE LOVED,

MY CHILD LONGS TO BE HUGGED,

MY CHILD NEEDS TO BE HEARD,

BUT WILL I LISTEN.

MY CHILD SEEMS TO BE LOST,

MY CHILD FALLS TO THE STREETS,

MY CHILD CAN'T SEE WHAT I SEE,

BUT WILL I LISTEN.

MY CHILD DOESN'T STRIVE TO DO HIS BEST,

MY CHILD WAKES UP AND COULDN'T CARE LESS,

MY CHILD HAS WROTE A NOTE ABOUT PUTTING A
BULLET IN HIS CHEST,

BUT WILL I LISTEN.

MY CHILD IS FEELING ALL ALONE,

MY CHILD IS SCARED TO COME HOME,

MY CHILD HAS LOST TOUCH WITH WHAT IS WRONG,

BUT WILL I LISTEN.

MY CHILD IS CONFUSED, ABOUT EVERYTHING HIS EYES HAVE SEEN,

BUT MY CHILD CAN ALWAYS COME TO ME, BECAUSE I WILL LISTEN

TO ANYTHING HE HAS TO SAY.

DEATH

Death
A lost memory for those left behind,
And the pictures of your face makes them cry" lost in a struggle or
battle of war,
The pain of your hurt lives on and on" the life for which is gone, or
is it the fate of
Love that's lost and gone.

Death
The passion you left behind, the touch of your hand is deeply
missed,
the kiss on the cheek or the way you said good night' or the
whisper in your voice when you'd softly speak, oh' and the way
we'd cuddle and make love between the sheets, it's
just the special part of you that lives inside of me.

Death
A life moves on 'the birth of a child, and the image of you has come
and gone.
The fires flame that holds your spot,
the vision of your face can be seen in this rock ,
the shape of your smile' the ways of your child, the missing of your
love
drives the mother wild "why my lord have you taken him away,
don't you know he's missed in every second of each day;

The love we'd shared was lost in one single fate;
But the hurt is strong and stays too long;
But everything you touch is left behind, and the
images of you are trapped deep within my mind

'' so everything we shared and all that was left,
It's the part of love '' and it' gets lost with your death.

This is dedicated to my Father-
Phillip Andrew Adams Sr.
also to my Stepfather-
Samuel Randolph Jordan

PIMPED IN THE STREETS

Silent cry's of remorseful bashing, taunting pleas of harsh
laughing;

Deep cry's of shameful teasing,
Touching and punching as the child crawls on her knees;
A whispering shout of hurtful screams,
The ignoring of mom as she lays to bleed;
The child's body is pulled back as she is continuously beat,
A holler of rage blurts out of her mouth,
The sexual abuse is never left out,
The tiny womb is ripped and torn,
The mercy of fright is a open door; strangest of pressure lies deep
In the child's mind, how could togetherness become a reason to
hurt someone,
The lost of time that comes with each day,
Trying to remember how it feels to see a smiling face"
The excuses she gives to protect her family,
Pretending she falls instead of sharing she's been beat;
The rest of life she jumps in her sleep,
Touching to her is a reminder to deep, So she ran away, and now
she's
being pimped in the streets.

DEDICATED TO ALL CHILDREN AFFECTED BY ABUSE!

PHANTOM

Phantom, of darkness eluding to sight and touch,
Abusing the limits of speed and stimulating your body with the
massive adrenaline rush:

The need to throw your caution: to the wind, the validation of your
spirit, and the expression of what you feel within, the always craving to
release yourself, the passive aggressive nature that you live behind the
need to be assertive,
And the one that always shine, the pressure of what your feeling and
the reason you need to rise: the phantom of all the madness: your
life has lived around, always ready to jump from lives big quest, the
falling of reality and the longing for passing the biggest test, the cry
to be heard and the need to be seen, the major attraction is all it really
means, phantom of danger" what is it all worth, the life you save might
just be yourself.

WOMAN WHO KEEPS MY HOME

MESMERIZING BLIST ENTRAPPED IN THE PASSIONATE
KISS,
LOST IN THE WEB OF SENSUOUS LUST AND WRAPPED UP
IN SPARKS OF SEXUAL REMINISCE;
INFLAMED WITH DESIRE AND ENTWINED FROM
PHYSICAL HEAT,
YOUR MIND GETS STUCK OR TRAPPED IN BETWEEN THE
SHEETS;
FOR THE FRAME OF BEAUTIFUL BLACKNESS,
AROUSED BY THE FORBIDDEN TOUCH,
THE STAINS OF JUICES ARE DRAINED;
FROM LOVINGS HUMPS; THE FEEL OF EMOTIONS ARE
COMPROMISED
BY SENSITIVE REASONING AND MOANS OF TIMELESS
RUSH,
THE TASTE OF YOUR LIPS ARE WEAKENING TO MY
KNEES,
THE EMBRACE OF GENTLENSS IS EXPRESSED THROUGH
STAGGEREN RIPS OF HUMAN FLESH,
SOFT BITES OF TEETH GRASPING AT THE SKIN,
THE WETNESS OF YOUR WOMB IS TASTING TO THE
TONGUES BITTER BUDS, THE POSITION OF THIGHS
SPREAD WIDE AND HIGH,
THE TOUCHING OF BODIES, ARE SWEATING TO
ROMANCE AND SEXUAL PANTS; THE BONDING OF ONES
BODY IS CARESSED BY STROKES OF WET AND MOIST
SKIN;
THE SMELL OF SEX LINGERS LIKE PERFUME, IN THE AIR,
THE AROMA OF LOVE AND PASSION NESTLING
UNDERNEATH THE NOSE, THE NATURE RISING TO

AROUSE THE EXCITEMENT FROM PLEASURES BLACKEST HOLE, THE LOVE WE'VE SHARED IS COMPASSIONATE AND COLD,
FROM LOVE'S PRIVATE DANCE,TO SOFTNESS MIXED WITH LOVE COMING FROM OUR SOULS,THE PUSHING OF DEEP HUMPS,THE SCREAMING OF PLEASURE CLIMAXES ALL STREAMS,THE RELEASING OF HEAVENLY JUICES CAPTIVATES COMPLEX BUT SWEET EMOTIONS, I HAVE TRAVELED THROUGH YOUR WOMB AND RESTED IN YOUR ARMS, I'VE FALLEN IN LOVE WITH THE WOMAN WHO KEEPS MY HOME..

WHEN GANGS BANG

GUN SHOTS RING " ACROSS THE NIGHT STREETS,
THE POLICE FIRE BACK, WITH THE GRAZE OF BLAZING
HEAT,

THE SHOUTS OF PAIN AS BULLETS PIERCE THE FLESH OF
BODY MEAT,
BLOOD DRAINS IN THE MIST OF CONTINUOUS RAPID
FIRE,

THE GANGS BANG FOR LACK OF FEAR AND THE
REQUEST OF THEIR FATAL RETIRE,
THE QUIET NIGHT BECOMES THE SPACE FOR ALL TO
HIDE, BUT GUN SHOTS COME FROM EVERY ANGLE AND
EVEY SIDE,

BUT GANGS CLAIM THE STREETS AND MURDER TURNS
INTO DAILY SUICIDE, THE GANGS FIGHT FOR POWER
AND SHOW NO COMPASSION FOR LIFE AS THEY EXPIRE,

THE RUSH FOR CASH IS THEIR CRY TO LIVE LIFE AS
THEY DESIRE, THE BULLETS FLUSH AND DESTROY
MASSIVE EMPIRE,
AND THE SHADOWS OF MADNESS BECOME A LITTLE
HIGHER; BUT GANGS

BANG FOR PEOPLE TO CALL THEM THUGS, AND THE
CHILDREN TO ADMIRE

AND SHARE THEIRS WITH REAL BIG HUGS; BUT BULLETS
SEEM TO NEVER

STOP, CAUSE WHEN GANGS BANG THE BODY'S WILL
NEVER STOP; CAUSE

WHEN GANGS BANG SOMEBODY ALWAYS GETS POPPED.

RAPTURE

You caught me the day you smiled" I was wrapped in your web and removed from the wild, I was enticed by your eyes and induced by infatuation and lust, I was putty in your hands I was grinded into dust, and you captured me with a wave and a hug" you touched my face and I fell in love, you said my name and sparks began to fly, you whispered in my ear, and my heart wanted to cry, for your beauty is taking my breath away, I get caught up in your passion everyday cause your rapture of love has left me with nothing to say, cause I'm caught up in your rapture and I can't find my way.

SHATTERED GLASS

Shattered glass upon my face, I can hear your voice, but my eyes won't open & all I see is dark space, shattered glass upon my face, my heart pounds at rapid speed, I search to find myself and to open my mouth to speak again, so the shattered glass I remain to lay in. Shattered glass upon my face, I arise to be moved to the emergency of time to patch all wounds, to encase broken bones and lie lifeless in a hospital room, so shattered glass upon my face, I hear your voice but I can't see your face, because my jaw is wired from the car crash, and I'm soooooo medicated, and the room is totally dim and my head aches from going through the windshield, so here I lay in the middle of empty space with shattered glass upon my face

TEARS THAT GET LEFT BEHIND.

A ring throughout the air,

A scream of mercy, followed by blurred vision and
Wide-eyed Stares,
Hollers of fright; screams of rage cut through the night air,
Puddles of blood drained in the streets,
The melting of skin, as bullets burn through the chunks of body
meat;
A graze of hollow points shadow drops of warm flesh falling onto
the narrow path,
Pools of body's drop like rain drops falling upon dry grass;
Cold chills creeping, as eyes begin to flash; stuttering tongues as
mouths speak blaze of bright light' shots whispering words to ears
are spoken the breathe that was there last'
Eyes filled with tears and comfort from death that comes to fast,
The bullets that ring out; come faster than lighting when storms
swirl down to crash,
The brisk cry for pleasures is the journey of ones we hide behind,
The loud bang is clinging inside the blank mind;
Because the string of pain is burned into the ends of time,
But nothing can ease or lift the tears that get left behind.

THIS POEM IS DEDICATED TO THE
OMAHA MALL SHOOTING TRAGEDY '07

*T*HROUGH *the* GLASS

Through the glass,

My eyes wander the pavement and the grass, I stare at the people walking,
And watch as time does pass, I admire the natures flash and the storms of lightening crash and I see all things through the glass"
Through the glass,
I relive my present from memories of my dreadful past, I see rebels of troubled times captured by problems that turn into a fight that becomes a fall out clash: that's what I see through the glass.

Through the glass"
I laugh as my reflections glares stares back at me, and my eyes get burnt from shines of bright sun light,
Splash through the glass as my heart beat becomes real fast and my pleasure has slipped out of my grasp, but my eyes travel through the glass.

Ms. COCAINE.

Ms cocaine, I fell in with you;
From the first blast, I kept you by my side in a tight grasp' I sniffed
you when I was

Down, and I smoked you when I was sad, I brought you home when
I was all alone,
Cause ms. cocaine never done me wrong.

Ms. Cocaine, pretty in color, I can find on the corner from the
hands of any brother,
Smoke you in my house and hide you from my mother, I can share
cocaine with a friend or a lover, cause ms. Cocaine is warmer than
a cover.

Ms Cocaine;

I cry when were apart, and I get pains in my heart, cause my life
is over if you're not apart, but the cocaine taste is still left in my
mouth, it lingers in my lungs and it burns in my chest, but I smoke
cocaine when I 'm going through stress, cause ms. cocaine has left
me a mess.

Ms Cocaine;

Has run me down, stole my life and turn my smile into a frown, it
has robbed me of my look and stole to many of my teeth, stripped
me of money and left me sleeping in the streets, cause ms. cocaine
has left me in grief.

Ms. Cocaine;

Doesn't love me no more, it ain't the same when she close the doors;
Cause cocaine is being sold from the drug store, and ms cocaine left
me for dead in the
Middle of the floor, cause ms cocaine is nothing but a whore.

Ms Cocaine;

I got the last laugh, moved on to rehab, I clean myself up, and threw
you all up, I no longer crave for powder up my nose, I look for snow
to fall from the sky, cause ms. Cocaine this is good-bye.

This is dedicated to ALL recovering addicts!

REFLECTIONS

I can see myself in the reflection of your eyes,
I can read the thoughts running through your mind'
I can hear your voice without you moving your mouth,
I can feel your tears before they fall down,

I can touch your lips without moving my hands'
I can see your beauty over and over again,
I can caress with your soul a million times, from one reflection in your
eyes' I dance with life whenever I'm next to you,
I feel piece of mind when I look at you' the reflection of love is in your
eyes, it's the stare from your eyes that has me hooked' and it's the
reflection in your eyes that makes me look, because I can see myself
in the arms of your soul" because the reflection in your eyes is a story,
over looked.

*L*OVE

LOVE LIVES IN YOUR HEART, BUT NOT IN YOUR FACE, IT CAN HIDE FROM YOUR EYES, BUT IT SHARES THE SAME SPACE, LOVE HEALS ALL PAIN, BUT IT CAN'T SAVE YOU, LOVE RUNS THROUGH YOUR VEINS AND IT SPEAKS IN YOUR SLEEP.

LOVE FALLS FROM THE SKY WHEN YOU'RE LOOKING THE WRONG WAY, IT DROPS IN YOUR LAP WHEN THERES NOTHING TO SAY, CAUSE LOVE HOLDS TIGHT WHEN YOU NEED IT THE MOST,WE'VE FOUND LOVE WITHOUT READING THE POST, CAUSE LOVE IS THE STRENGTH THAT MOST PEOPLE WON'T SHOW.

LOVE IS A CRY WHEN YOU'VE LOST ONE OF YOUR FRIENDS, IT WILL PROTECT YOU SOMETIMES AND OTHERS IT WILL DO THEM IN, LOVE PLAYS IN OUR HEADS OVER AND OVER AGAIN,CAUSE LOVE BURNS AND SOMETIMES STINGS, BUT LOVE JOURNEY'S THROUGH YOUR DREAMS.

LOVE REWRITES ALL OF OUR STORIES, BUT LOVE LIVES INSIDE OF ALL OUR DREAMS, BUT THE BEST PART OF LOVE, IS THAT IT SAVED ME.

M.A.K.I.N.G . LOVE .

Making Love ''
It's not it's not, the way you hump'' It's about the soft caress or the way
you touch, the smoothness of her skin''
Or the way you kiss her lips over and over again, it's about looking into
her eyes or nibbling on her tongue inside your mouth,
Making love:
is real when you're holding her in your arms' or kissing her neck, to the
soft moans,
Making love:
are the passionate pleasures ready to be served, to the rhythmic,
rhythms or twist, bumps and turns, to spread her legs and let your
tongue explore between her thighs and then ride up and down her slit,
and then suck softly on the rising of her clit, as you enjoy the juices her
body releases'' and then you taste each nipple as they peak back at you
'' as you journey inside the wetness of her womb,
you begin to share motions, of passions' which is real love''
but it's not about the hump until you stop or the pump until you drop,
and it's the pleasure of our bodies in a hot sweaty gridlock,
and the warmth of the gentle tease' the taste of your passion, as I ride
up between your knees'' the toying of simple play, the laughter of how
deep we fade,
from moment to moment'' and touch to touch, from kiss to kiss and
from hump to hump'' because making love, is about the embrace of
each others minds ''as well as sharing the pleasures of your body and
mines.

MIND

Say ye"

Oh my precious queen, why has thou love been pushed apart,
I must touch;
I must feel" our love was special and still remains real,
has thou been burned by the bitter flame,
has thou heart been crushed by guilt and shame"
for there is no pain that we can not get through,
for the hurt I feel is when I 'm not with you"
my eyes shed tears and my heart sorrow;
but it's our love that, lives through out tomorrow"
for in my dreams I feel your touch,
I kiss your lips and savior the rush" for in my eyes are visions of
you,
And where are thou cries"
When I see the moon"
As the stars peek at me, and the sky holds your smile"
And the pleasure of love when one stares into your eyes;
Say ye" one more time, where is thou love"
It's so hard to find, but one place I look, it can never hide"
Your love is here and it stays in my mind.

REMEMBERING DAY'S

Remembering day's of a less stressful time, when life was easy and fun wasn't hard to find, where compassion was given and I was a star that had to shine, because I dropped some things along the way, but I'm still remembering the days.

Remembering the day's of drifting or running astray" Doing things with the family and listening to the words they say, being a friend to those who have stumbled along the way, and most of all I put my feelings on display" because remembering the day's.

Remembering the day's I struggled just to get by, I was afraid to fall asleep and my shame made me cry, I was lost in all my dirt and my worth was pushed aside, I am a man who loves my yesterdays, but I can't walk away, from all that comes my way, because I still love just remembering the day's.

REBELLIOUS

REBELLIOUS DAYS WHEN MY FIGHT WAS STRONG, THE GAME I LIVED THOUGH I KNEW IT WAS WRONG,

MY SILENT STEPS WERE TRAVELED HARD AND LONG, AND MY CRY'S WERE CRIED WHEN I WAS ALL ALONE, A BORN THUG NEVER

TO STRAY AWAY, I'VE BEEN JUMPED IN THE STREETS AND ON THE GROUND I LAID, I STALKED NIGGAS WHO NOW LIE IN THEIR GRAVES, AND I BATTLED WITH BROTHERS WHO'S NAMES I'D RATHER NOT SAY AND I'VE LAID IN BLOOD AND TO THE LORD I'VE PRAYED, I REBELED AGAINST PEOPLE WHO STILL REMEMBER MY FACE, AND I DREAMED AT NIGHT THAT I GOT LOST IN THE WRONG PLACE, BUT TODAY I LOOKED IN THE MIRROR AT MY OWN FACE AND I THANKED THE LORD FOR GIVING ME GRACE, BECAUSE NOW MY LIFE IS ON ITS PACE TO REBEL RIGHT NOW I CAN'T LET THAT BE MY FATE.

SING ME A SONG

SING ME A SONG OF LOVE NOTES AND PASSIONATE
QUOTES THAT LINGER IN MY EARS, SING FROM YOUR
HEART AND GLARE INTO MY EYES AND WORDS COME
WITH PROVOCATIVE STARES, A HARMONY FILLED
TUNE THAT CLINGS IN MY MIND, THERE ARE WORDS
AND PHRASES THAT GET LEFT BEHIND, YOUR SONG
HAS TOUCHED EMOTIONS THAT NOBODY COULD EVER
FIND, SO SING ME A SONG ONE THAT BLOWS MY MIND.

SING ME A SONG, ONE OF LUSTFUL COMPRIMISE A
REASON TO ALL MY QUESTIONS, AND THE EXCITEMENT
OF LOVING ME WITH THE STRENGTH FOR THE TEARS
I CRY, BECAUSE THE SONG YOU SING IS THE HUG THAT
HOLDS ME AT NIGHT, SO SING ME A SONG THAT WILL
LEAD ME THROUGH FOGGY NIGHTS. SING ME A SONG,
YOU KNOW THE ONE I LOVE TO HEAR, THE SONG THAT
SITS IN THE NIGHT AND SHINES LIKE A STAR SO SING
ME A SONG THAT WILL HUG ME LIKE YOUR ARMS.

BETWEEN THE SHEETS

Oh my nature is rising and my thoughts are only of you, the wetness of your pussy and the sweetness of your juice oh how I miss the passion in your kiss, your tongue's touch and the way your hands play as you caress my manhood and gently rub and massage the stiffness of my cock, your drip of wetness as your mouth awaits all that is not alive,

your moans escape as your pussy drains with each touch of my finger, the warmth of your breath up against my flesh and the timeless expression your face does hold, the rises of my nature as it enters your womb, oh my humps are bumps and the pleasure becomes ecstasy" as our bodies embrace in sweat from the passion of lover's heat, our climax is the melody of sweet music as we reach our peak between the sheets

*H*USTLER

I'M A HUSTLER, AND THE STREETS ARE ALL I KNOW,

I'VE MADE MY SHARE OF FRIENDS BUT I'VE BATTLED A
LOT OF FOES, I'M A HUSTLER"
I TAKE MONEY FROM WEAK PEOPLE, AND EVERY
WOMAN IS A BITCH OR HOE, BECAUSE I'LL DO
WHATEVER FOR THE MIGHTY DOLLAR AND I DO WHAT
I DO.

I'M A HUSTLER" I'M NOT AFRAID TO DESTROY YOUR
LIFE, AND I'LL SELL YOUR WIFE A DIME, AND I'LL
SEX HER BODY DOWN FOR PAYMENT TONIGHT. I'M A
HUSTLER" I'LL TEACH YOUR KIDS THE GAME, AND MY
HEART WON'T FEEL NO SHAME, CAUSE I'M A HUSTLER
WHO WEARS THE BLAME, AND I FEEL YOUR EYES GLARE
BUT I'M A HUSTLER WHO FEELS NO FEAR,

AND I'M THAT HUSTLER WHO LAUGHS AT ALL YOUR
CRYING TEARS.

WISPERING

WISPERING WINDS WHIRL AROUND THE OCEAN BLUE,

THE SUNLIGHT GLARES FROM BETWEEN THE CLOUDS,
THE BRISK SMELL OF ROSES GROWN AND THE STENCH
OF RAIN LINGERS,

AND THE WAKEFUL EYES CAPTURE THE RUSTIC
MORNING VIEW,

I GET THE FLASH OF QUIET MELODIES, AND LONG
LASTING MEMORIES, STRONG WAVES OF WIND BLOW
ALL OVER ME, AND THE SILENT CRASH OF FALLEN
WANT TO BE'S, BECAUSE THE WISPERING WINDS WHIRL
UNDERNEATH THE SEALING WINGS UP HIGH AND THE
SONG FROM THE EARTH'S CENTER, AND THE WANTS
FOR NOTHING AND TIME'S ENDLESS QUEST, TO ROB
FROM ME,

wHAT LIFE HAS PROVIDED AND GAVE ITS BEST TO SEE
FOR THE WHIRLING WINDS HAVE CLEANED MY EYES,
BECAUSE THE WISPERING IN MY EARS IS COMING FROM
GOD.

In THE SHADOWS

LOST BEFORE ANYONE CAN FIND ME, AND STUCK IN A
ROOM WITH NO WALLS,

BUT REACHING HANDS CAN'T CATCH ME FROM WHICH
I BEGIN MY ETERNAL FALL, WITH NO LIGHTS TO GUIDE
ME, MY HEARTBEAT COMES BUT SOMETIMES PAUSE,
THE SOUND OF VOICES TALKING HAVE BEEN LOST TO
WIND BLOWING AND HOLLERING FILLS MY EARS, AS
MY VOICE SCREAMS OUT EACH CALL, THE DARKNESS
EMBRACES ME AND I CAN'T FIND ONE FACE, BUT THE
FLASH OF WHITE LIGHT HAS CARESSED ME

IN THE SHADOWS of THE FLASH OF EMPTY SPACE, AS MY
BODY LIES MOTIONLESS ON THE FLOOR, I'M STILL LOST
IN THE SHADOW OF DOPE RUNNING THROUGH MY
ARM.

TOUCH ME

Touch me one more time,
Don't hide from me, what you hold in your
Mind, I can handle your sweet release and to you
I will let you shine,
and for all your emotions'
your love is still one of a kind, and massage me
with your words; comfort my soul, with each vocal lyric released from
your soft but beautiful lips,
let's journey through compassion; as if we were entwined in a
passionate lovers kiss;
for what do you hold inside of your heart that in time it would not be
shown,
that's why I say touch me one more time,
for you can console' all that I am with all that I have given 'so touch
me one time' because of you 'my life can now be lived.

CLOWNS

Time and time again you say you don't hate'

But rage is the stage, I see in your face; but you hate for no cause;
And your life has no pause,

You're a clown' with a smile painted upside down;
You toss in your sleep afraid of what you just might see,

you take no risk on who you want to be/ you say my color is alright
with you but you speak my words, as if you can do what I do, and you
never stop to understand why I would never want to be like you, you're
a stranger to a world "where love has shut you down, but please believe
you can't find a way to turn your life around because hate is your life,
and you can be found in a place of old retired clowns.

WATCH ME DIE

LOOK INTO MY EYES AND WATCH ME DIE,

FEEL MY PAIN, AND WATCH ME CRY, OH YEAH AND

LISTEN TO ME LAUGH AS I STARE AT LIFE'S FATAL

CALL, ERASE MEMORIES AND START MY LAST CRAWL,

WALK THROUGH THE STAINS AND DRAINS ALL THAT

LIVES INSIDE, HOLLA FOR REASONS I JUST MIGHT DIE,

SO HEAR I LAY ALL ALONE WATCHING TEAR DROPS

FALL FROM MY EYES, AS THE WALLS CLOSE AND MY

MIND BEGINS TO STALL, RESTING MY FOOTSTEPS ON

EACH STEP I TAKE, AS YEARS BECOMES MONTHS AND

MY AGE BEGINS TO WALK AWAY, I CAN HEAR MY

HEARTBEAT PAUSE THROUGH MINUTES OF THE DAY,

WATCH ME DIE, I'M SORRY I CAN'T STAY.

RIGHT DUDE

MY LOVE" It's your sarcastic tones, and your angry words that have left me wondering" are we in love, or is being with me something you find time to do,

oh my love, I drain my heart to you" I release how I feel, but you turn your back to kiss me off to hell, I've listened to your cries and believed your every word,

I show love to your pain, but you walked away from my opened arms, now my love" what more can I do, I've given you the best of me", but nothing is ever good for you" but I wish you all the best, when you find the right dude.

FROM DADDY WITH LOVE

Asia" A gift sent to me from God, the face that I see" and I know you were created from love" you are the reason I know that God watches from up above", and this is from Daddy with love.

Asia" I lost my heart along the way, but your love is locked in my soul, an d I have so much I want to say" to you, I cherish my every waking day" and I love and thank God above, and this is from Daddy with love.

Asia" You're apart of me" and I dream of the day when I can hold you in my arms and kiss you on your cheek, but until then I thank God above, and this is from Daddy with love.

MEMORY

Stolen Moments" flush by memories of brutal pain, captured by
moments of past or present shame" lasting scars and torn down
melodies,

they play in songs that remind me of what I use to be; the rash splash
of whispering voices surround my inner being" I pretend to ignore
but refuse to claim that anyone is talking to me, the stolen time I left
behind"

the memories still seem to haunt all that I use to be; I laugh in my
head, but can't sleep and I toss and turn in my bed" because my stolen
moment has become a memory that is now dead.

THROUGH THE EYES OF A CELL

THROUGH THE EYES OF A CELL, FOUR WALLS PAINTED TAN, NO HEAT TO WARM YOU, AND YOUR SHEETS ARE DIRTY AFTER BEING WASHED AND RETURNED WITH SPOTS AND BAD SMELLS, NO ROOM TO MOVE BECAUSE OF NOT ONE BUT TWO PEOPLE IN A CELL; PICTURES HUNG STAINS OF CUM SPOTS, LADIES WITH LEGS OPEN,DICK HARD AS A ROCK ,WAR STORIES BEING SLUNG, LICKS OF OLD SONGS BEING SUNG,PICTURES OF PRETTY GIRLS AND A MAN WANTS ONE, THE STAGGEREN SIGHTS OR VIEWS SEEN FROM THE WINDOWS, SPOTS ARE LEFT BEHIND FROM SPIT DROPPINGS FROM CONVERSATIONS THAT GOT HEATED OR HOT,FROM EARS ON THE WALL STORIES BECOME CONCULUSIONS AND DECISIONS BECOME LOST, THROUGH THE EYES OF A CELL, LIFE JUST WASTE AWAY, YOU LOOK FOR BRIGHTER MEMORIES, BUT PAIN JUST GETS IN THE WAY, FOR THROUGH THE EYES OF A CELL, EVERY MAN IS ALONE SUFFERING IN HELL.

THANK YOU

THANK YOU" FOR CARRYING ME FOR 9 MONTHS, FOR
BRINGING ME INTO THE WORLD AND NURSING ME TO
PERFECT HEALTH, FOR GIVING ME ALL THE THINGS
YOU KNEW I WAS GOING TO NEED, AND THANK YOU
FOR BEING A MOTHER TO ME!

THANK YOU" FOR COMFORTING ME WHEN I WAS IN
PAIN, FOR SHELTERING ME WHEN I WAS YOUNG AND
REMOVING MY HURT WHEN TIMES GOT TOUGH, AND I
THANK YOU FOR LOVING ME SO MUCH.
THANK YOU" FOR HELPING ME GROW UP IN POSITIVE
SIGHT, FOR SHOWING ME THE WAY IN THE EARLIER
PARTS OF MY LIFE, AND I THANK YOU, FOR MAKING ME
STAND UP FOR WHAT IS RIGHT.
THANK YOU" FOR BEING THE MOTHER OF LOVE,
AND SHARING THE KNOWLEDGE THAT PULLED ME
THROUGH THE LIGHT, AND I LOVE YOU WITH ALL MY
MIGHT.

I AM A MAN

AS I TAKE THIS PEN AND BEGIN TO WRITE, THE
STATEMENT IN MY HEART HAS NOT BEEN FOLLOWED
IN MY LIFE, A DESPERATE CRY HAS FALLEN SHORT,
BUT I CAN'T PRETEND, THAT MY VOICE HASN'T BEEN
IGNORED, BUT ALL FORMS OF EXPRESSIONS PRECEIVE
TO LINGER ON, BECAUSE IN MY HEART I RETREAT TO
MOVE ON, I AM A MAN AND I WILL BE STRONG.

AS I CRY TO MYSELF, AND RETHINK ALL MY THOUGHTS,
I LEARN TO ACCEPT ALL THE THINGS THAT GET LOST
IN MY THOUGHTS; CAUSE ALL I SHARE IS DESTINY'S
LONG TRAVELS, AND I TREASURE ALL OF LIFE'S
PRECIOUS JOURNEYS AND THE STRENGTH I HOLD IS
DEEP IN MY SOUL, AND I STRIVE TO SURVIVE ALL THAT
GOES WRONG, BECAUSE I AM A MAN AND I WILL BE
STRONG.

...WOMAN

..WOMAN WHAT ARE YOUR COMPLAINTS, THAT I AM A DOG, AND YOU FEED ME STEAK, DID I MOVE TOO SLOW OR ARE YOU LIVING OFF BATE, DID YOU FALL TOO HARD OR HAS SOMEONE CLEANED YOUR PLATE.

..WOMAN WHY ARE YOU STRONG, BECAUSE THE PAIN AND THE HURT YOU HAVE SURVIVED, WHAT ABOUT ALL THOSE YEARS YOU TOLD YOUR LIES, OR DOES THAT NOT MATTER TO THE SOULS YOU HAVE MADE CRY, OR ARE THE FALLEN STONES JUST MERE ALIBIS, COULD YOU BE TO BLAME, OR HAVE YOU TOO MUCH PRIDE TO FEEL THE SHAME.

..WOMAN WHAT MAKES YOU BETTER THAN ME, BECAUSE YOU HAVE BREASTS OR A WET MUFFIN BETWEEN YOUR KNEES, WHY SHOULD I APOLOGIZE, FOR THE MISTAKES YOU MADE WHEN YOU RAN OVER ME, BUT I DON'T CRY I JUST DIG DEEP INSIDE AND REMOVE THE LEECHE FOR NO WOMAN CAN CRUSH MY HEART, THEY JUST MAKE IT SKIP A BEAT.

*W*HAT USED TO BE

SO MANY THOUGHTS OF MY CHILDHOOD PASTS, AND
OF THE LOVE THAT CAME BUT NEVER LAST SO WHY DO
THE TEARS FALL SO FAST, AND THE MEMORIES OF YOU
JUST SEEM TO FLASH, LIKE THE WANDERING HEARTS IN
OUR MEMORIES AND THE CHERISHING DAYS, OF WHAT
USED TO BE.

WHAT USED TO BE. LOVE IS WHAT WE'VE NEVER SEEN,
AND THE RAINDROPS FALL LIKE A SOFT MELODY, AND
YOU CAN NEVER RUN AWAY FROM YOUR PAIN BUT LIFE
WILL REMAIN THE SAME, AND THE NIGHTS BECAME
THE MEMORIES OF WHAT USED TO BE.

WHAT USED TO BE. WHEN THE SILENCE IS ALL AROUND,
AND THE FEAR THAT CREEPS INSIDE, AND THE
DARKNESS THAT TURNS YOUR HEAD, AND THE HURT
THAT LIES NEARBY, FOR YOUR EYES ARE SO ENRAGED
FROM THE YEARS OF HEARTACHE AND PAIN, SO MANY
EMPTY MEMORIES, AND YOUR HEART IS FILLED WITH
SHAME, TRUE LOVE IS WHAT WE WANT TO ACHIEVE,
AND THE IMAGES OF WHAT USED TO BE, WHAT USED
TO BE.

*L*OVE..

LOVE
LOVE IS AWARE, DEVOTED TO SOMEONE AND NEVER LEFT
UNPREPARED, LOVE IS STRONG TO THE BONE, AND ALWAYS
READY TO DO GOOD THINGS, AND KEEP IT TRUE.

LOVE
..IS BLAMELESS AND SO NOT AFRAID, SO KIND TO OTHER
PEOPLE AND NEVER BLINDSIGHTED BY SIMPLE MISTAKES,
LOVE IS SUCH A STRONG WORD, IT'S A STAR IN THE SKY
AND…IT RAINS DOWN ON YOUR HEART.

LOVE
IT NEVER HAS TO EXPLAIN, THE REASONS ARE
UNDERSTANDING AND PERCEIVING ALL WISHES AND
GRASPING THE CHANGING OF OUR WAYS.

LOVE
CRYS BY YOUR SIDE, SHARES PAIN IN YOUR ARMS, AND
PROTECTS YOU FROM HARM, LOVE IS REAL AT ALL TIMES,
IT DOESN'T MAKE FUN AND IT WON'T CRUSH YOUR HEART.

LOVE
SHINES LIKE THE MORNING SUN BUT AS LONG AS I GOT
YOU YOUR LOVE IS NUMBER ONE.

BEST FRIENDS

SEÑORITA, DO YOU MIND IF I SPEAK TO YOU-CAN I
ADMIRE YOUR BEAUTY AND PARTAKE OF YOUR SWEET
SMELL THAT'S UNDERNEATH MY NOSE, CAN I FEEL THE
TOUCH OF YOUR SOFT BUT WARM HAND,

CAN I EMBRACE YOUR WORDS AS THEY'RE SPOKEN
FROM YOUR LIPS, DO YOU MIND IF I FALL INTO YOUR
STARE-WOULD YOU LIKE IF I TOUCH YOU OR RUN MY
FINGERS THROUGH YOUR HAIR, CAN I CARESS YOUR
MIND AS WELL AS YOUR TIME,

CAN I SIP FROM YOUR ESSENCE AS IF IT WAS A GLASS OF
WINE, SEÑORITA, DO I MAKE YOU FEEL INFECTED BY
MY WORDS, OR DO I ENTICE YOUR INNER BEING BY THE
WAY I SLING MY SPEAK,

CAN I PROLONG FOR A MINUTE AND SUCK IN THE TONE
OF YOUR VOICE, CAN I STARE INTO YOUR EYES AND GET
LOST IN EVERY NOTE-DO I MAKE YOU FEEL LIKE SAYING
MY NAME, DO I HOLD YOU IN MY ARMS AND MELT YOU
LIKE A FLAME- SEÑORITA, I'M YOUR BROTHER, LOVER
AND YOUR BEST FRIEND.

$\mathcal{P}$ROCLAIM

MY LOVE, WHY ART THOU, INFLAMED BY BITTER KISSES,
HAST THOU BEEN CAPTURED, BY LOVE'S LOSSES AND
LIFE'S SOUR DISHES, ART THOU LESSER THAN ALL PAIN
SUFFERED HAS MY HEART BEEN CRUSHED, BY STONES
AND WASHED UP WISHES, OH SAY THEE, ART THOU
CRIES FALLEN ON DEATH EARS, DOES MY PAIN OR HURT
LINGER AND SPREAD THROUGH THE STENCH OF STALE
AIR, CAN WE MOVE ON FROM THE PRESSURE OF LOVE'S
ROTTEN PASTS, FOR MY LOVE HOLDS NOTHING BUT
MEMORIES OF HEARTS THAT DROPPED FROM ONE TOO
MANY STABS.
MY LOVE, WHY AM I LOST, TO LIFE'S SEVERE PAST,
HAVE I COME TO SURRENDER, OR FALL TO HEARTLESS
THOUGHTS AND TIMES ENDLESS CRASH,

MY LOVE, WHY ART THOU EYES FILLED WITH TEARS,
AM I CONFUSED BY ALL THAT WE'VE SHARED, OR HAVE
I BEEN TORTURED BY THOUGHTS THAT COME AND GO
AND MINDS DRIFTING FLASH.
MY LOVE, I HAVE YET TO FEEL WHAT HIDES, I LIVE FOR
THE DAY YOU SHARE WHAT'S BEHIND THE SOULS OF
YOUR EYES, YOUR LOVE IS COLD, BUT REMAINS TO BE

UNTOLD, FOR THY PAIN IS SHARED, BUT NEVER
REALIZED. OH MY LOVE, WHAT DOES THOU SAY,
SHOULD I RUN, OR PRETEND YOU'RE NOT HERE AND
SHADE MYSELF FROM DAYS OF BEAUTY AND LOCKED
AWAY FROM THE SUN.

MY LOVE, WHERE ART THOU HOLLOW WORDS BEING

SPOKEN, SING TO ME, BELIEVE IN LOVE AND LEAVE MY HEART UNBROKEN, FOR THOU HAVE NO DAY, OR NIGHT WHERE SHAME HAS NOT ENTERED INTO MY LIFE, MY LOVE RELEASE THEE FROM THE BITTER FLAME, GRASP MY HEART, AND CARESS ME FROM LOVE'S WORTHLESS GAME, PROTECT MY HEART FROM THE GIFT MY LOVE LONGS TO PROCLAIM.

My BOO

SHADED PICTURES OF THE LOVE OF MY LIFE, THE
DREAM OF MY HEART AND THE SEED OF MY SOWN
OATS, THE PASSION OF LOVE SHARED BY TWO HEARTS,

THE EXPRESSION OF SEXUAL FIRE FUELED BY TOUCHING
ONE ANOTHER, BURNING DESIRES ENTICED BY AROMAS
UNDERNEATH THE BRIDGE OF MY NOSE,

THE CLINGING OF DEEP FEELINGS AND PARTING
EMOTIONS THAT REMAIN TO SHOW THE CHILD OF
PLEASURES, A GIFT THAT JOURNEYS AND FOLLOWS THE
PATH AND ROADS THAT DIRECTED OUR PAST, TO EYES
OF COURIOUSITY, AND SEARCHING TO FIND THE RIGHT
PATH TO ALLOW THEMSELVES A BRIGHTER WAY,

THE CHILD OF LOVING, BECOMES THE FACE YOU SEE
EVERYDAY, BECAUSE LIFE IS THE TREASURES SHARED
THROUGH THE LOVE WE HOLD FOR YOU, YOU'RE THE
GIFT TO ME AND YOU'LL ALWAYS BE MY BOO.

Time

TIME: HAS REMOVED ME FROM THE CRUST OF THE
WORLD, IT HAS ERASED THE MEMORIES AND REPLACED
THEM WITH IMAGES OF FILTHY AND DIRTY DREAMS.

TIME: HAS SHED ALL OF MY EMOTIONS, CHANGED MY
SPIRIT AND PARTED MY HEART AS IF IT WAS THE OCEAN,
TIME CLAIMED MY SOUL AND TWISTED MY FLESH AND
LEFT ME BITTER AND COLD.

TIME: CAN'T CHANGE THE FLAWS OF WORDS THAT
SCARED YOUR MIND, TIME CAN'T HIDE THE WAY
OTHERS SEE YOU THROUGH THEIR EYES, TIME CAN
ONLY CHANGE THE WAY WE LIVE OUR LIVES, CAUSE
TIME CAN HOLD YOU AND SCRATCH EVERY VERSE AND
LINE.

TIME: IS THE DAYS WE WASTE WITH NOTHING TO
SAY ITS LATE HOURS OF NIGHT AND BRISK MINUTES
IN THE EARLY DAY, ITS LOVE WE SHARE AND ITS PAIN
THAT LIVES INSIDE YOUR SOUL WHEN YOU'RE LOST
SOMEWHERE IN YOUR SLEEP OR DRIVING HOME ALONE
ON A DARK SWIRLY ROAD, CAUSE TIME IS THE REASON
ALL MEN STAND ALONE.

FRIEND OR FOE

FRIEND OR FOE, A BROTHER FROM JAIL GOES HOME FROM A THREE FLAT ABOUT ONE YEAR AND HE COMES RIGHT BACK, WITH TALES OF THE STREET EMBEDED IN HIS HEART, ABOUT BROTHERS FROM THE HOOD THAT DIDN'T PLAY IT SMART, THEY CAUGHT CASES IN MIAMI, NEW YORK AND LITTLE BRICKS AND SOME MADE FRONT PAGE FOR KEYS OF COCAINE, DOPE AND GUNS AND THE BROTHERS CALLED IT GETTING PAID, BUT MANY BROTHERS GET THEIR BODIES LAID IN A GRAVE, CAUSE OF THINGS THEY DIDN'T LET GO, SO IS THIS YOUR FRIEND OR FOE.

FRIEND OR FOE, A BROTHER COMES HOME HOT FROM THE SPOT, STRAIGHT TO THE BLOCK AND SLINGING THAT CRACK ROCK, BUT THE STREET CLOSED DOWN AND THE COPS COME AROUND AND HE GETS SWEPT UP ON THE DROP, AND THE STAIN OF TEARS TRACK ON HIS FACE AND THE LIGHT POPS ON AND HE WAS OUT OF PLACE, BECAUSE THE THOUGHT CAME DOWN AND MAYBE HE SHOULD HAVE KNOWN IS THIS MY FRIEND OR FOE

STAY

BLOOD ON HANDS, EYES FILLED WITH TEARS, A BODY ON THE GROUND AS PEOPLE STOP AND STARE, SCREAMS OF FRIGHT, LIGHTS TURNED DOWN LOW,

THE STREETS ARE FLUSHED WITH DARKNESS AND THE SOUNDS OF GUN FIRE CONTINUE TO BANG ON, THE AROMA OF BURNT FLESH CARRIED THROUGH THE NIGHT BREEZE THE PUDDLES OF WARM BLOOD SEEPS INTO THE CRACKS OF BROKEN CONCRETE,

THE FIRM CARESS, THE LONG EMBRACE, THE CLINGING TO HOLD ON TO LIFE'S LAST BREATH, THE MOON LIGHTS SHINES TRACES OUTLINE THE MOTIONLESS BODIES, WHY RUNS THROUGH YOUR MIND EVERY TIME YOU FALL ASLEEP, BECAUSE THE BLOOD ON YOUR HANDS SEEM TO NEVER WASH AWAY, AND THE HURT IN YOUR HEART STILL LIVES ON TO THIS DAY, BUT THE MEMORIES YOU HOLD, ARE HERE TO STAY.

PROMISES

I PROMISE TO ALWAYS STAND BY YOUR SIDE TO PROTECT
YOU FROM THE EVILS THAT LIE IN THE SHADOW OF THE
NIGHT, I AM THE MAN WHO WILL LOVE YOU AND GUIDE
YOU WITH ALL OF MY MIGHT,
I WILL LEAD YOU BY YOUR HAND AND EMBRACE YOUR
BODY TIGHT WHEN TROUBLES OR PAINS LINGER IN
YOUR HEART I PROMISE TO BE THE MAN TO ERASE ALL
YOUR PAINS.
I PROMISE TO NEVER DISRESPECT YOUR HEART I
PROMISE TO PROTECT YOU FROM THE PEOPLE THAT
CHERISH WORDLY PROCESSIONS AND COULD CARELESS
ABOUT YOU AS LONG AS YOU PLAY YOUR PART,

I PROMISE TO SHADE YOUR EYES FROM THE IGNORANCE
THAT LIES IN THE DARK, I PROMISE TO BE YOUR BEST
FRIEND ALWAYS NO MATTER WHAT I WILL LOVE YOU
IF YOU ARE IN NEED OR WETHER YOUR SOUL IS AT
FULL SPARK, I PROMISE TO BE YOUR FRIEND WHEN IT
RAINS AND STORMS, I WILL BE YOUR PROVIDER, YOUR
COMFORTER AND WE'LL RIDE THE WAVES OF LIFE HAND
IN HAND AND I PROMISE TO ALWAYS BE YOUR LOVER
AND YOUR BEST FRIEND.

FOR I PROMISE ONE MORE TIME TO BE THE MAN THAT
YOU NEED THROUGH GOOD AND TROUBLED TIMES FOR
BABY GIRL I PROMISE TO GIVE YOU THE GIFTS OF LIFE
AND SHARE THE RICHES THAT EVERY MAN HAS IN THIS
WORLD FOR I PROMISE TO ALWAYS TREAT YOU AS MY
DIAMOND OR MY PEARL.

DEAR GOD

DEAR GOD LET ME PRAISE YOU WITH OPEN ARMS, I'M ON ONE KNEE AND I'VE OPENED UP MY HEART, I PRAY TO YOU ABOUT ALL MY TROUBLED TIMES,

I RELEASE MY SOUL WITH NOTHING LEFT BEHIND, I CRY TO JUST SHOW I'M IN DEBT TO EVERY DROP OF BLOOD YOU'VE SHED, FOR EVERY BLESSING YOU HAVE GIVEN AND THE PRICE YOU LIFTED OFF MY HEAD, AND FOR THE MERCY YOU HAVE BEEN ABLE TO SHARE, I LOVE YOU, FOR GIVING ME STRENGTH FOR NEVER TURNING YOUR BACK ON ME, AND NEVER LEAVING ME FOR DEAD,

DEAR GOD YOU HOLD ALL THE GLORY AND YOUR BEAUTY IS WIDELY SPREAD AND MY HEART BELONGS TO YOU AND TO YOU I OWE ALL MY PRAISE.